10 SILLY CHRISTMAS JOKES FOR KIDS

Jess Kiddin

BLOOM BOOKS
FOR YOUNG READERS

Published by:
Bloom Books for Young Readers
an imprint of Ulysses Press
PO Box 3440
Berkeley, CA 94703

978-1-64604-562-4

Printed in the United States by Versa Press
2 4 6 8 10 9 7 5 3 1

Image credits: cover © Ori Artiste/Shutterstock.com;
Santa © Elizaveta Parfinenko/Shutterstock.com;
patterns © Marina9/Shutterstock.com

Why go down the chimney?

It soots me.

What does a snowman eat for breakfast?

Frosted Flakes.

What does a vampire snowman give you?

Frostbite.

**How do elves
learn to read?**

They learn the elf-abet.

What do you call a really old snowman?

A puddle.

What's the only thing a snowman can smell?

Carrots.

What did the gingerbread man use when he twisted his ankle?

A candy cane.

What is Santa's favorite toilet bowl cleaner?

Comet.

Why is a Christmas tree so good at sewing?

It's full of needles.

Where does Santa go on tropical vacation?

Ho-ho-waii.

Who delivers presents to all the fish in the sea?

Santa Jaws.

How do the elves get back to Santa's workshop?

In minivans.

Why do Christmas trees smell so fresh?

They're covered in orna-mints.

Why is it so cold on Christmas?

Because it's in Decembrrrrrr.

Why does everyone love Frosty the snowman?

He's so cool.

What do you get when you put an apple on a Christmas tree?

A pineapple.

What language do they speak at Santa's workshop?

North Polish.

What is it called when Santa stops his sleigh?

A Santa pause.

What is a rude reindeer called?

Rude-olph.

Why can't Santa spell "holidays"?

He has noel.

Where do gingerbread men keep their money?

In the snow bank downtown.

What do grumpy sheep say to each other on Christmas?

Baaaaaa-humbug.

Knock, knock!
Who's there?
Avery.
Avery who?

Avery merry
Christmas to you!

What did one Christmas tree say to another?

Lighten up!

What month does a Christmas tree hate the most?

Sep-TIIIMBERR.

When Santa takes attendance, what do the elves say?

"Present!"

Who goes "Oh, Oh, Oh"?

Santa walking backward.

What's red, white and blue on Christmas Eve?

A very sad candy cane.

Knock, knock!
Who's there?
Donut.
Donut who?

Donut open until
Christmas!

How much did Santa's sleigh cost?

Nothing! It was on the house.

What do you get when a duck dresses like Santa?

A Christmas quacker.

Who was the Christmas tree's favorite President?

Wood-row Wilson.

How can you tell Santa has been in a room?

You sense his presents.

What's the name of the dog at the North Pole?

Santa Paws.

What do strawberries sing on Christmas Eve?

Tis the season to be JELLY.

What game do reindeer play at parties?

Truth or deer.

What's the only thing at the table on Christmas that isn't hungry?

The turkey—it's already stuffed.

What type of music do they listen to in Santa's workshop?

Wrap.

What's the only Christmas present you can't beat?

A broken drum.

**What types of sheets
do gingerbread men
have on their beds?**

Cookie sheets.

What does Santa wear after Christmas?

A soot.

What is the ornament's favorite subject in school?

Chemis-tree.

What do the reindeer think of Santa's singing?

He sleighs.

What costume did Rudolph wear on Halloween?

A cari-boo.

How did the Christmas tree get ready for the party?

It got spruced up.

What's Santa's worst nightmare in a chimney?

Getting claus-trophobic.

Knock, knock!
Who's there?
Justin.
Justin who?

Justin time for presents!

What does a snowman have when it's upset?

A meltdown.

Knock, knock!
Who's there?
Ho Ho.
Ho Ho who?

**Your Santa needs
some work.**

What is the name of Santa's mean cat?

Santa Claws.

How do elves cheer on Santa?

Sant-applause.

Where do reindeer get coffee in the morning?

At Star-bucks.

What's Frosty's second-favorite breakfast cereal?

Ice Krispies.

What candy is Santa's favorite in Texas?

Jolly Ranchers.

What was Santa called when he didn't have any money?

Saint Nickel-less.

What is Santa's favorite flavor of ice cream?

Sugar plum.

What's Santa's favorite way to drink Cokes?

Through Santa straws.

Who is the elves' favorite singer?

Elfish Presley.

Why do elves make such good friends?

They're never s-elf-ish.

What are the rules at the North Pole called?

The Santa Laws.

Knock, knock.
Who's there?
Dewey.
Dewey who?

Dewey know how long
until Christmas?

**Knock, knock!
Who's there?
Mary.
Mary who?**

Mary Christmas!

Knock, knock!
Who's there?
Chris.
Chris who?

It's Christmas, silly!

Where does the Christmas tree keep its things?

In its trunk.

Why are toys so good at meditating?

They're always in the present.

What's a Christmas tree's favorite shape?

A tree-angle.

Knock, knock!
Who's there?
Interrupting Santa.
Inter. . .

**HO HO MERRY
CHRISTMAS!**

What did the wise man say after giving the frankincense?

Hold on, there's myrrh.

What does Santa say when the elves finish getting the presents ready?

That's a wrap!

Why was the stocking so smelly on Christmas?

It had a foot in it.

How does Santa start a sleigh race?

Ready, set, ho-ho-ho!

Why did the Christmas cookie stay home?

It's feeling crummy.

What did Frosty say when Santa parked in front of his house?

There's snow parking here!

What is the elf's least favorite thing about school?

All the gnome work.

What is Santa's favorite old movie?

Rebel without a Claus.

Why did Santa invite Snoop Dogg to the North Pole?

He's so good a wrapping.

How do Spanish-speaking sheep say, "Merry Christmas"?

Fleece Navidad.

What did the Christmas tree say to it's shaggy neighbor?

You need a trim.

What's the snowman's favorite lunch?

Chili.

What's the snowman's favorite dinner?

Icebergers.

Why is the Christmas tree at the dentist?

To get a root canal.

What kind of car does Santa's head elf drive?

A Toy-ota.

What is the toucan's favorite Christmas song?

Jungle Bells.

What do you call an elf wearing ear muffs?

Anything you want, he can't hear you!

What falls a lot but never gets hurt?

Snow!

Where did Frosty learn to cut a rug?

At the Snowball.

What is Santa's favorite state in the U.S.?

Idaho-ho-ho!

How do you know Santa's good at karate?

He's got a black belt.

What snack did Santa bring to the Super Bowl party?

Crisp Pringles.

How did the turkey learn to play in the band?

She used her drum sticks.

Why did Rudolph have to repeat fifth grade?

He went down in history.

Why is Santa so good at gardening?

He loves to hoe!

What do you say to scare an Advent calendar?

Your days are numbered.

What amphibian lives at the North Pole?

The mistle toad.

How come the snowman can't get anywhere?

He never learned to ride his icicle.

Why did the turkey make such a good pillow?

It's stuffed!

How do Santa's helpers take photos?

Elfies!

Why is a snowman so good at losing weight?

He just has to wait for spring.

What's the most common wine at Christmas?

Ewww, brussel sprouts!

Why was the
icicle so upset?

His friends were all flakes.

What happens when you give Santa's helper a compliment?

You boost its elf-esteem.

Where does Rudolph keep his schedule?

On the calen-deer.

What is every dad's favorite Christmas carol?

"Silent Night."

Add Your Own Jokes!

_____

_____

_____

_____

_____

_____

_____

_____

_____

_____

_____

_____

_____

Merry Christmas!